W9-BSR-491

Principles of Design
Pattern

THE DESIGN CONCEPT SERIES

Elements of Design
TEXTURE George F. Horn
COLOR AND VALUE Joseph A. Gatto
SPACE Gerald F. Brommer
SHAPE AND FORM Albert W. Porter
LINE Jack Selleck

Principles of Design
BALANCE AND UNITY George F. Horn
CONTRAST Jack Selleck
EMPHASIS Joseph A. Gatto
MOVEMENT AND RHYTHM Gerald F. Brommer
PATTERN Albert W. Porter

Principles of Design
Pattern

Albert W. Porter
Professor of Art, California State Unversity
Fullerton, California

DAVIS PUBLICATIONS, INC.
Worcester, Massachusetts U.S.A.

To Shirl, Kim and Todd

Copyright 1975
Davis Publications, Inc.
Worcester, Massachusetts U.S.A.

Printed in the United States of America
Library of Congress Card Number: 75-21113
ISBN 0-87192-077-8

Printing: Davis Press, Inc.
Binding: A. Horowitz & Son
Type: Optima Medium
Graphic Design: Penny Darras, Thumbnail Associates
Consulting Editors: Gerald F. Brommer, George F. Horn,
                    Sarita R. Rainey

10   9   8   7   6   5   4   3   2   1

Contents

Introduction

The word pattern is multidimensional. It can refer to a life style, a paper layout for an article of clothing, a shifting population or types of behavior. In visual terms, it is easy to state and use. The key to understanding is another word, repetition. When something is repeated with sufficient regularity, a pattern is created.

But understanding the word is only a start in seeing both the significance and visual qualities of pattern. We need

to recognize pattern for what it can do for adding visual zest to living and as an important compositional principle.

This book is part of a team effort to discover the art principles in our environment. Emphasis, Contrast, Movement and Rhythm, Balance and Unity are companion books that will show how each principle operates in life around us. The five sections of this book look at planned and random pattern, basic types of pattern, patterns associated with materials, patterns in nature and patterns put to use.

Most of the photographs in this book were taken in the urban areas of Los Angeles, California, and suggest the many prospects each of us has to discover patterns in our own environments.

Patterns Everywhere

Wherever we look, we are certain to see some form of pattern. Patterns are everywhere; on the clothes we wear, in the food we eat, around us in our homes, in city life, throughout most of nature and in many of the objects we use.

Pattern, the repetition of units or motifs, provides us with a wealth of information. It tells us about the structure of things, it reveals surface qualities, reflects the use of materials and the variety of processes used

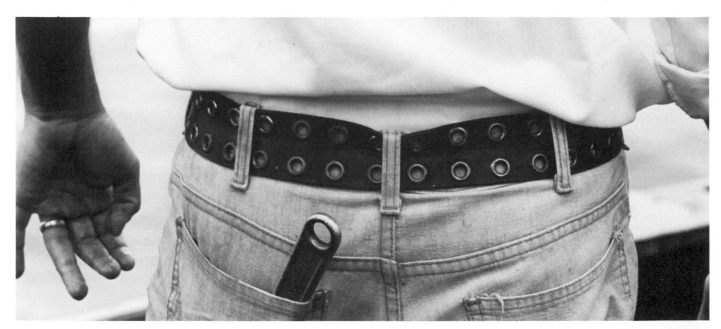

with materials and even helps us visually measure an object or area.

For our purposes, pattern has two important functions. One is to organize or unify an area or object; the other is to provide visual enrichment and enjoyment. Because of this, pattern is a versatile tool for the designer, architect, artist and craftsperson.

The patterns in these photographs point out some of the variety we experience in seeing pattern. The dense compact cluster of cactus plants contrasts with the dancing free form pattern of light and dark of the water in the swimming pool. A leather belt utilizes regularly repeated hole units for decoration, while the feeling of speed is captured with the circular patterns on a car's hubcap.

Our first goal is discovery; looking to see the many ways patterns are formed and used in our lives.

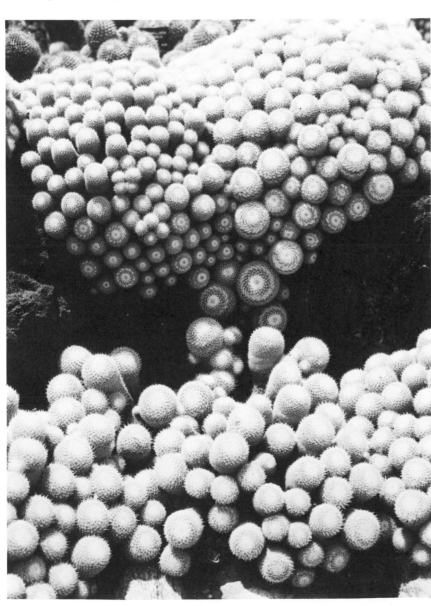

PLANNED PATTERN

Pattern can be thought out and created in a systematic and organized way, or may occur accidentally in a random fashion.

Planned pattern, whether manufactured or natural is precise, measurable and consistent. In the brick patterns, we see two examples of skillful pattern usage which produce visual unity and variety. Note the effective placement and spacing of bricks. A surface of a brick wall starts to lose its uniform pattern through removal, weathering and paint.

11

Nature is a master designer when it comes to pattern development. Most of natural pattern is purposeful, that is, to help itself survive or adapt to life. This honesty of pattern usage is the most exciting aspect of nature's artistic intent.

The turtle's hard crusty shell derives strength and beauty from its segmented pattern. Even the thick skin has its unique pattern, designed to add improved resistance to wear and tear.

Zebras are speedy animals that might find some comfort from the camouflage offered by the striped pattern

which can visually fuse with its African environment. For us, the pattern has a strong optical quality that seems to move.

This crab's shell points out a planned pattern's premise, regular repeated units. Each leg segment repeats itself in a uniform fashion with both sides formed of identical units. We call this arrangement a symmetrical pattern.

Another camouflage pattern that easily identifies its owner. See how beautifully the pattern fits the form of the giraffe and adjusts itself to the size and shape of body, leg and tail sections.

RANDOM PATTERNS

Random means by chance or without purpose. Many patterns just happen, caused by accidental arrangements or produced without consistent design. Random patterns are usually asymmetrical (not identical on both sides), non-uniform and irregular. Those conditions make random patterns visually exciting and expressive. The absence of planning is their charm.

The footprints in the sand came about from a casual grouping of prints. The pattern has some common factors, foot shape and textured soles, along with sand texture and indentation.

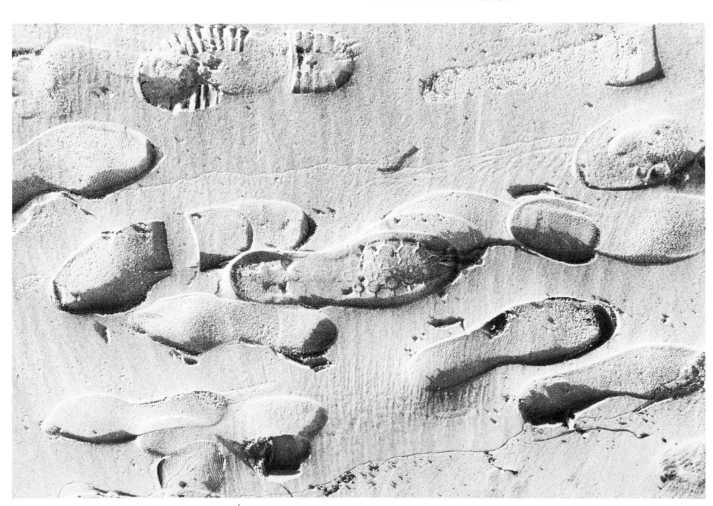

Cyclists enjoy the random patterns of light and shadow cast across a concrete pathway. Autumn leaves add to the effect.

These dried tar drips form lineal random patterns on a beach wall. The pitted surface also contributes its own random pattern. The resulting effect is a rich surface pattern that has a wide variation of dark and light areas and strong dominant blacks to capture attention. This wall section approaches some of the effects sought by contemporary painters who use accidental or random paint patterns to create pictorial interest.

The ripening process on bananas brings out the random arrangement of brown flecks, similar to the sun's capability of producing freckles.

A look into a dishpan of agitated suds can reveal random patterns of bubbles that come close to being uniform as they pile up along the upper edge.

The enemies of wood, such as termites and weather, create intriguing random patterns that can completely alter a surface. The results often form strong design patterns. Water erosion has a way of producing its own distinctive pattern on rock and sand surfaces.

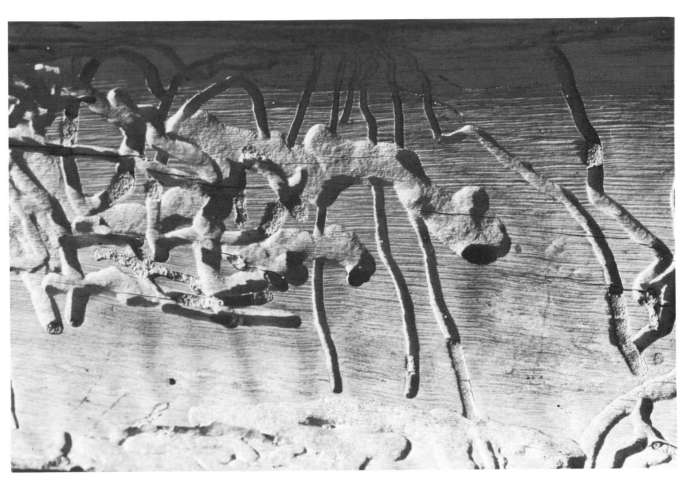

17

Basic Pattern Arrangements

MOTIFS AND REPEATS

A motif is a single unit that, when repeated in a uniform fashion, forms a pattern. The water bureau's metal

cover is a disc motif that we see producing a sidewalk pattern as it repeats itself in regularly spaced intervals. Even within the disc-motif unit itself, we can observe a uniform pattern of small pyramid shapes. Each pyramid motif has been repeated at regular intervals.

Artists John and Marian Scott have used circular motifs to form a porch screen. These two metal units show how different approaches can be used in developing a pattern theme.

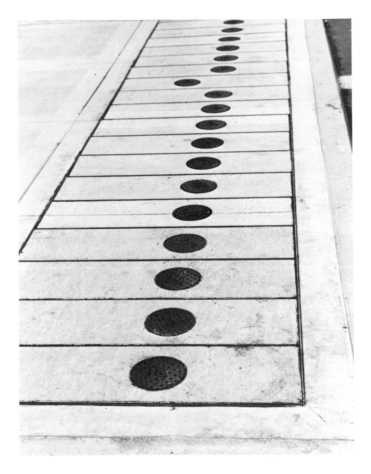

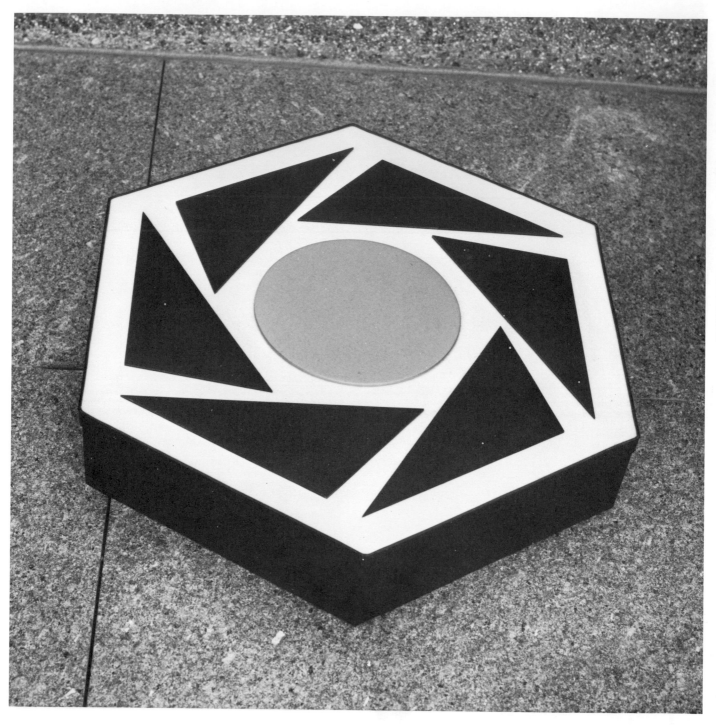

A motif, like this triangle, can be skillfully positioned so that a pattern is produced which has strong eye-catching qualities. A California banking service identifies itself with this simple dynamic pattern.

Line up some mailboxes and you have a simple repeat pattern.

In the interest of safety, a bus bumper takes on a patterned look. The motif shape of each protruding unit, decorated with studs and a metal strip, repeats itself to create a three-dimensional pattern.

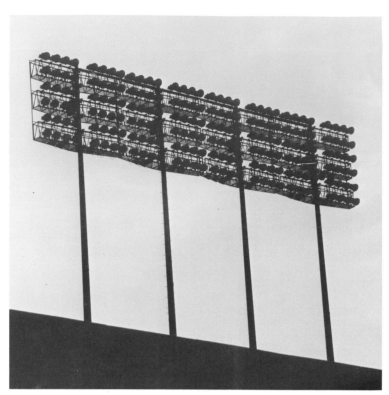

LINEAL PATTERNS AND GRIDS

One of the easiest patterns to discern is the grid, which is formed by a regular network of lines or shapes. We see grid patterns in a variety of uses—gridirons or football fields with regularly spaced lineal units to mark off the yards, checkerboards, automobile grills, waffle

This lighting structure for a baseball park is a grid pattern of repeated light units and lineal metal structure supports. The total pattern forms a long rectangular shape.

A woven lineal grid of metal bars protects a tractor's radiator. Here is an example of pattern overlaying pattern.

irons or the grids formed by city streets intersecting each other.

A handsome ceiling grid allows either daylight or artificial light to illuminate a large art museum complex. Its lineal grid heightens the feeling of space as we observe each succeeding unit appearing smaller as it goes away from us.

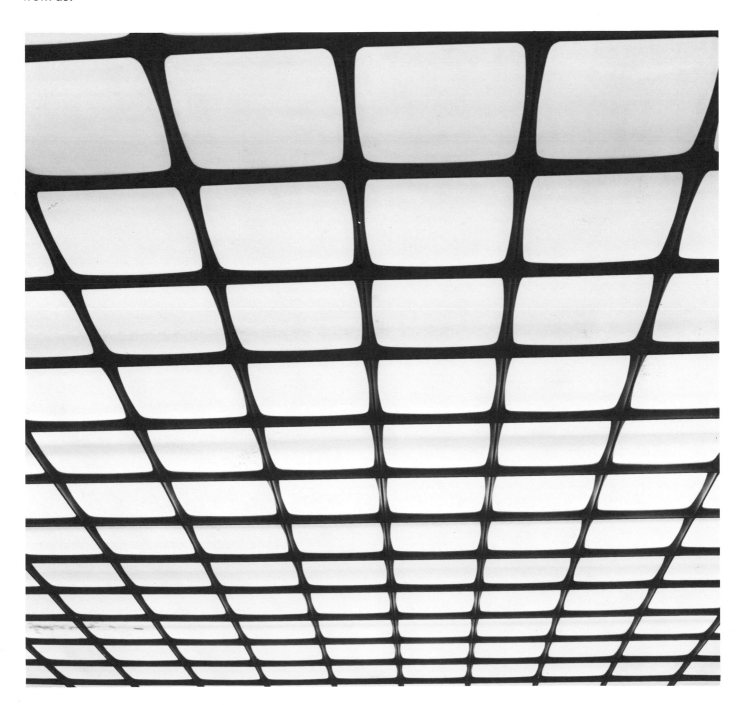

HALF-DROP AND ALTERNATING PATTERNS

By moving an element or motif halfway back or down from each other, a modification on the grid pattern occurs which gives both variety in spacing and an active pattern quality. We sense a visual movement as we look at half-drop patterns or patterns where the motifs alternate in position.

Streaking across the sky, this flying formation of the Thunderbirds, a special acrobatic unit of the U.S. Air Force, produces a simple half-drop pattern.

Cactus leaves alternate in layers as an aspect of their growth pattern. This pattern produces a spatial movement through its alternating stacking arrangement.

A university's architect created a handsome three-layered walkway structure by alternating each pillar-support unit. Notice the interlocking shapes of the covering masonry, which makes an undulating pattern as we scan the walkway forms.

An alternating set of case displays for dried beans produces a pattern of varying textures and values.

RADIAL AND SPIRAL PATTERNS

Radiate means to branch out from a central point. Star shapes, asterisks, wheel spokes, fireworks bursting in the air are radial patterns produced by an extension of each element or lineal unit from the center outwards, usually in precise intervals or spaces. Radial patterns have an explosive quality and seem to accelerate our eye speed as we follow the enlargement of shapes as

Citrus fruit, cut into halves, reveal radial patterns of pie-shaped wedges.

Windmill vanes radiate in an angled arrangement to catch the wind, and to also catch our eye with its strong visual pattern.

Look at the precise radial pattern of the structure of this carnival ride.

they move outwards. We can generally describe radial patterns as being dynamic, active and structurally strong.

Spiral patterns are created by a coiling action which occurs around a fixed axis or imaginary central line. These kinds of patterns produce strong, rhythmical visual actions.

Coil springs are spiral forms that, when repeated, produce spiral patterns.

This staircase gains grace and a pleasing visual path by its spiral pattern of repeated curves.

BORDERS AND BANDS

From clipper ships to sport cars, patterns are used to decorate the surfaces of the things we use. These added designs offer a sense of elegance and individuality. Often, no expense is spared to enrich surfaces. The border or band of repeated motifs is an easy way to provide added beauty, as seen in these examples. A swirling border of scroll-like shapes on the front of this

sailing ship reflects a similar pattern of wave action below. Automotive striping or banding is now common practice both to personalize cars and visually suggest speed and power. Four vertical bands of intricate motifs add both protection and aesthetic qualities for a window area. A structure that was once used for housing horses and carriages in Southern California has given its wall surfaces added visual status with bands of three-dimensional and cut-out patterns.

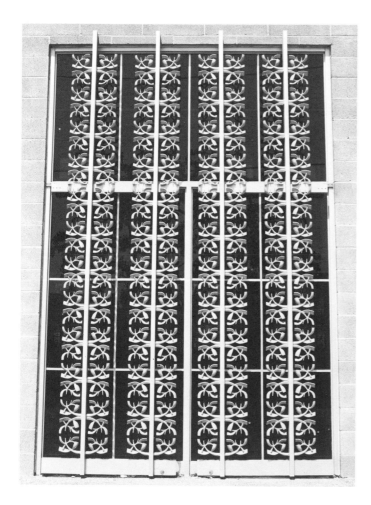

RHYTHMICAL PATTERN

Rhythm and movement team up to produce a wide variety of pattern in our lives, whether it is a musical score, a gracefully repeated design or a captivating slice of nature. Rhythmical patterns flow easily from one unit

to another. The visual beat of rhythmical patterns moves
us along forms or across surfaces in smooth uninter-
rupted paths. As you view these photographs, note the
variety of rhythmical patterns caused by such diverse
items as architectural design, rippling sand waves,
driftwood or the sweep of jets in flight.

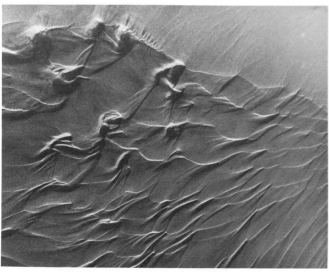

Pattern and Materials

Often, a pattern is produced either by what something is made of or by how it is put together. Wood has an entirely different look and feel from steel, as fabric from glass or clay from plastic. Each of these materials has its own special qualities which deal with its surface, its strength or plasticity and how it can be used. We can stack bricks, bend thin strips of wood, mold clay, weave strands of fiber or pour concrete into forms. The result will be some type of pattern formation that relates to the materials used and the structural methods employed.

SURFACE PATTERNS

Surfaces not only create patterns because of their material composition, but, also, by how those surfaces are treated. A surface may be smooth, such as a glass tumbler, a ceramic bowl or a painted wooden wall. If we etch the glass, press designs into the clay or stipple the paint, we have changed the surface for a patterned effect. Surfaces are enriched by texturing, pressing in designs, raising or lowering surfaces, manipulating with various tools and even allowing the surface to weather naturally.

A breeze blowing through a plastic-curtained building construction site causes a surface pattern of stretched and extended forms.

Molds are efficient ways to reproduce similar products. A waste paper container, using a pressed-in, alternating pattern, has both an unique appearance and a functional use.

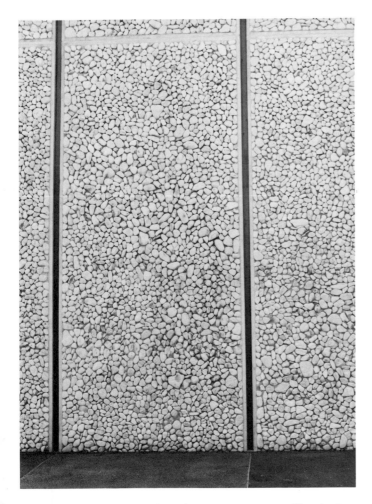

A large wall of textured surface pattern was effectively produced by the use of rocks and concrete made in casting forms. The separating spaces create a repeat lineal pattern.

Fastening metal pieces with rivets has given this railroad car a textural surface pattern of lineal rectangles.

The relief wall surface, created by positioning blocks of wood in varied horizontal or vertical arrangements, produces an attractive sunlight modulator. Each recess or protrusion casts its own shadow to further enhance the surface design.

Aging paint cracks into a pattern of line and shapes. The gaps formed by flaked-off surfaces add interest and contrast.

Interpace Tile Co. mass produces wall tiles which can be arranged in large or small decorative units. Variations in color and value introduce more pattern possibilities. Photography by Jack Laxer.

Ceramist John Harding has tooled a line pattern into a clay jug for surface enrichment.

STRUCTURAL PATTERN

One major user of pattern is architecture. Since architecture tends to be precise, its patterns are generally sharply defined, geometrically based arrangements. By repeating building forms (whether they are posts, windows or boards) at constant intervals, a strong pattern is

produced. The two structures on the facing page demonstrate this theme. A water tower, with its converging cylindrical supports and strengthening cross braces, makes a powerful uniform pattern. A distinctive geometric grill (repeating triangular shapes) has been superimposed over a window grid to gain a rich patterned look on this building facade.

Concrete beams provide both support and structural pattern to this university building. The recessed, square-unit shapes under the roof give added pattern effects.

A perspective pattern of pier posts moves our eye seaward as each receding unit appears to move closer together.

Looking at the great variety of structural pattern applications around us reveals unending pattern possibilities. Steel rolls for concrete pillars, welded steel sculpture, interwoven wood slats, wire fencing and window treatments are a small sampling of patterns formed by structural devices.

DECORATIVE PATTERNS FROM MATERIALS

Seeing pattern possibilities from how a material looks, or can be used, has always intrigued humans. Even the caveman seemed to need images painted on walls and ceilings to bolster his spirits. It is a natural response to decorate or visually improve our surroundings by arranging materials into pleasing patterns.

Parts of telephone poles and huge timbers form new spatial patterns for a concrete walk.

Wood grain has its own unique decorative pattern. Weathering or treating with oils or stains can intensify the "grained" look. Grains are often matched to unify a patterned surface. This piece of outdoor fencing has a rustic appearance produced by weathering along with streaks caused by rusting nails.

Wood can be sawn, shaped, sanded and nailed or glued together and also arranged to form patterns. We see on these pages a number of pattern developments from using wood to solve decorative needs.

A more primitive approach to building a fence and corral gate has produced a pattern structure that fits the forming process.

The "tailored" look of a picket fence contrasts with the informal look of the corral structure and is a result of precisely-cut pieces nailed at regular intervals. White paint and strong sunlight increase the power of the pattern.

Shaped shingles have been carefully applied to a wall surface to create an alternating pattern. An overhead beam arrangement superimposes its own decorative shadow pattern.

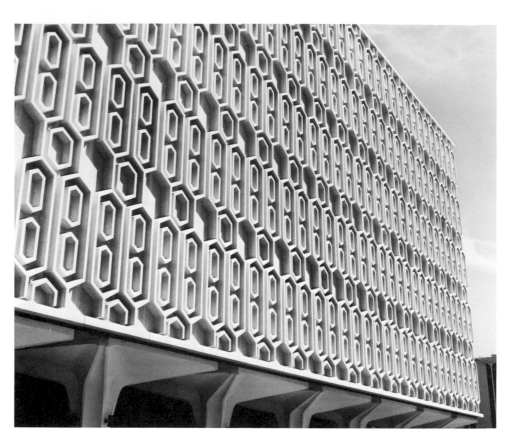

A visually-demanding relief surface of concrete covers this university library building in Fullerton, California.

The use of smooth dark rocks embedded in concrete is widely used to produce overall pattern.

One strong pattern dominates this shopping center entrance and is skillfully echoed in quieter patterns of tile on the walkway.

If privacy isn't needed, pierced concrete block forms can produce decorative walls that separate areas but allow air and light passage.

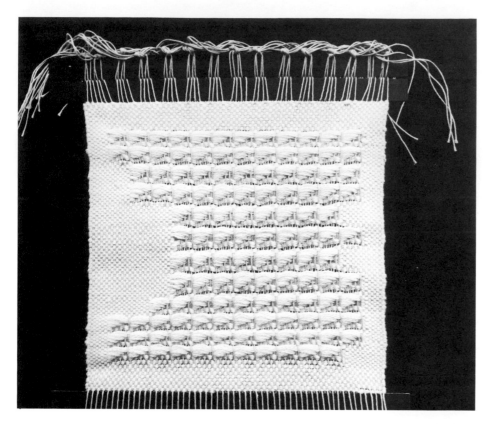

Clint MacKenzie is a fiber artist who utilizes the richness of woven and crocheted materials to achieve unique, beautifully executed patterns.

Handsome decorative patterns are a result of arranging, weaving and tying in this Japanese bamboo wastepaper basket.

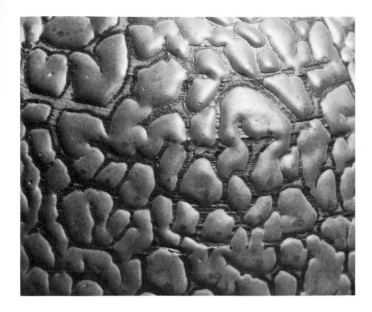

A look at a section of glaze on a ceramic pot reveals an overall decorative random pattern of raised glaze surfaces contrasted against a stained form.

Raul Coronel painted a series of patterned leaf shapes with glaze and colored slips to achieve a decorative composition for a ceramic bowl.

This small detail of a wooden stool by Sam Maloof discloses the attractive pattern of grained wood.

Patterns in Nature

SYMMETRY

If one were to divide nature's patterns into two general categories, one could use the terms symmetrical and asymmetrical. Symmetry means equally balanced, with each side matching each other, using an imaginary center line as a point of reference. Symmetrical patterns achieve a sense of beauty and order because of this even matching of the art elements. Asymmetrical patterns take on a more adventurous look; they are active,

unevenly matched, yet often balanced, and irregular in their use of the elements.

A tree and cabbage leaf are startlingly similar in their symmetrical look. Branching forms move outwards from a central axis and present a strong, balanced pattern. Animal life is widely arrayed in pattern formations, both symmetrical and asymmetrical. The peacock's plumage, both front and rear views, makes a visually-active radial pattern that is symmetrical. Its feathers carry out the same theme.

ASYMMETRICAL PATTERN

The "unalike" look of asymmetrical forms in nature results in patterns that are dynamic and moving. Even the irregular spacing of a simple tree stem causes an active pattern because of its asymmetrical placement of twigs and buds.

A group of cactus shapes forms a highly irregular and
asymmetrical pattern. Most of the action is to the right.
Some counter-balancing forms move in an opposing
direction.

PATTERNS IN OUR LANDSCAPE

Both nature and humans have a way of improvising with pattern formations. Rock walls fractured by weather and pressure, lineal patterns in a field of vegetables, waves moving in on the Oregon Coast, plowed patterns of land or the soft look of rolling hills demonstrate the

Silhouetted patterns of palms and cloud formations help to romanticize a part of Hawaiian landscape, while, below, tourists enjoy a spectacular light-and cloud-pattern show during Greece's twilight hours.

Artist Jim Alford uses his camera to focus in on a panorama of dramatic cloud patterns and light designing itself on the Pacific Ocean.

50

wide variation of patterns that are a part of our visual landscape.

Nature is resplendent with patterns. These patterns provide visual enrichment that delight the eye, as well as provide a never-ending resource for artists and designers.

PATTERN DETAIL IN NATURE

Close inspection, whether by the camera's lens, a magnifying glass or plain eyesight, reveals many patterns that often go unnoticed. The richness of detail in pattern in nature is available for anyone willing to take

time to observe closely. Bob Burningham's wondrous color photos on the opposite page bore into the center of a flower to uncover exciting pattern formations, as does his study of the textured pattern on a strawberry. Nature offers a great variety of pattern detail options, such as the radial line pattern on the top of a pumpkin.

The isolation of a single section for careful scrutiny makes the discovery of patterns a visual adventure. A cabbage leaf has its own unique textural pattern of undulating folds and a supporting branching structure. A palm tree's trunk can be studied for its interweaving pattern. A small part of a dandelion flower will offer a delicate lineal composition.

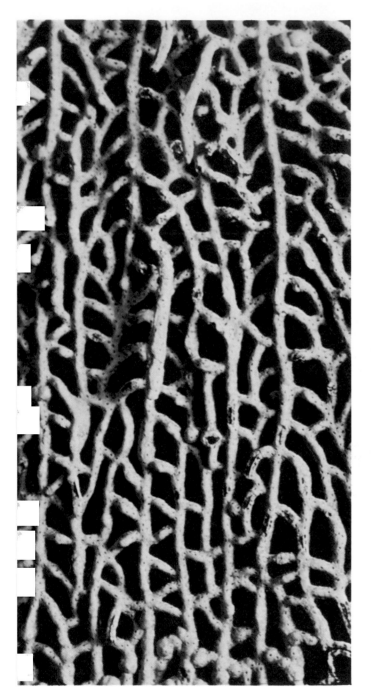

We see in these photographs the striking contrasts that patterns produce in nature—the irregular grid formation of seaweed, the elegant precise rhythm of a chambered nautilus shell, the swirling designs in a tree fungus and the very subtle decorative patterns in a segment of a butterfly's wing.

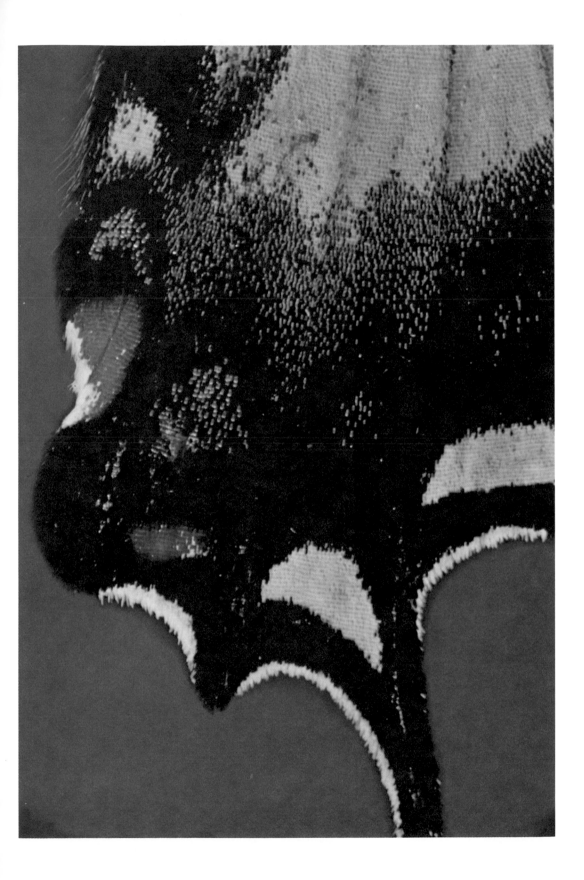

One may look over a section of landscape and select the pattern details that arrest the eye. A frozen pond with its light-textured surface, the wispy pattern of delicate tree forms or the soft pattern of snow-covered rocks, all offer detailed investigation. Even the way water drips and freezes can suspend a pattern of translucent forms of irregular edges and ridged shapes.

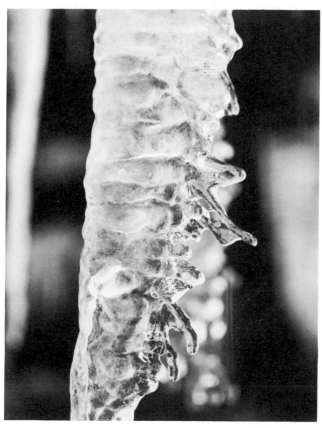

Pattern and Design

The treatment of fabric design is almost unlimited. Clothing or manufactured yardage reflects the ingenuity of the designer in organizing patterns to produce effects. The poncho from Guatemala uses a zig-zag pattern for striking results and the richly patterned fabric, created by the Marimekko Company in Finland, offers customers endless possibilities for use. Marimekko designs, courtesy of Design Research Corp.

The two words, pattern and design, seem inseparable. If you create a pattern, you have produced a design. If you make a design, it will often use pattern. Design has much wider applications and covers very broad human areas, such as environmental design or architectural design. Pattern, in one way or other, will usually be part of the design process.

Hang gliding achieves more glamour when the glider surfaces are enriched with brightly colored patterns. Photograph courtesy of Don Dwiggins.

DARK AND LIGHT PATTERNS

The fireworks bursting over Disneyland, the fractured pattern in glass shadows or the filigree metal design in a church door, all have one overriding design quality—powerful dark and light patterns. Dark and light contrasts make a pattern readable and visually demanding, especially when those contrasts are extreme.

© Walt Disney Productions

A table and bench are hard to discern because of the cast shadow pattern. Pattern can help to destroy the identity of a shape.

Sunlight falling across forms or shadows cast on surfaces yield pattern configurations that have their own design qualities. Pipes demonstrate this situation as the circular shapes of the pipes have been modified by sun and shadow patterns.

Painted dark and light patterns also achieve unusual effects. The stylized figure shapes activate a wall surface to help advertise a clothing store.

A supporting wall for a freeway has been enlivened with a forceful design pattern that capitalizes on dark and light contrasts.

PATTERN FOR USE

The desire to decorate is innate. Enrichment by pattern has been one of the most used visual devices to achieve decorative effects. Putting pattern to use takes on two distinct aspects; one is to make something look better, the other is to make it function better. Often appearance and function, working together, produce the best designs.

Personalizing a small store's wall with a king-sized portrait has a function in identifying a location, but its intent is primarily decoration.

Marimekko fabrics are well known for their bright, bold patterns and elegant designs. Some of the processes used to produce these materials include the artist's ideas and layout, the silk-screening of the design and final assembling. These fabrics can then be reshaped into clothes, upholstery material, pillow covers, bedspreads and wall hangings. Both function and decoration are considered. Photographs courtesy of Design Research Corp.

Our homes are one of the areas of living where patterns function best. If we live in a highly populated housing development, the mere repetition of living quarters produces a pattern — similar walls, roofs, tiles, windows, all add to the creation of pattern. Indoors, we can

Photograph courtesy of Interpace Tile Company.

be more selective. We can choose the patterns with which we want to live. Our patterns may be tile for a playroom, a rich lively pattern of fabrics for a kitchen or a more formal use of pattern for a dining room. Even our side tables can add pattern enrichment.

Kitchen and dining room photograph courtesy of Design Research Corporation.

Architecture has come a long way since the Bradbury Building was built in Los Angeles before the turn of the century; yet, its widely acclaimed use of pattern is still around, taking on new forms. A large grill pattern of pressed metal hides a parking lot in the opposite photograph. Tiles decorate the front of a hotel in Hawaii. The lineal patterns of concrete design buildings in downtown Los Angeles. A large aviary enclosure used radial structures and netting to house its exotic birds.

Bradbury Building, Los Angeles, Calif.

Hilton Hotel photograph, courtesy Interpace Tile Co.

The functional use of pattern is all around us. A power pylon's insulators create patterns by how these units were constructed and assembled. Even the wires themselves, loops and straight lines, form a pattern. Arranging lights for a fountain and the placement of water nozzles produced the circular pattern. Tires come from molds that press out a tread pattern, and flattening the loose ground for a freeway requires a pattern of steel prongs on an earth-conditioning machine.

Patterns can decorate surfaces, help us park our cars, make it easier to find the ketchup in the supermarket or organize window units. Pattern's versatility is its major contribution to better living and increased visual enjoyment.

INDEX

These bells ornament a wall with a pleasing pattern of dark and light rhythms.

Acknowledgments

The tops of uncooked spaghetti are just one of a kitchen's store of patterns.

A simple dark and light outfit provides visual relief from a heavily patterned bench.

First of all, my thanks to Davis Publications for leadership in producing this design series. Their staff have been very supportive in bringing these important concepts to fruition. Jerry Brommer has always made our paths smoother, and his help has been an important contribution to this series development.

A number of people were generous with photographs. My gratitude goes to Dr. Bob Burningham for excellent color shots, to Don Dwiggins for the hang glider photos, to Joe Gatto, John and Marian Scott for some nice additions and to George Horn for getting our vision off the ground with aerial views. Clint MacKenzie supplied important help with fiber designs. Jim Alford provided the ocean view.

Design Research Corporation aided considerably with photographs (particular thanks to Anne Cushman and Jan Kagihara), as did Interpace Tile Incorporated. Thanks to the Flying Thunderbirds of Nellis Air Force Base for their formation photos. Levi Strauss Inc. (Beth Altschul was most helpful) supplied numerous photos of their Levi design contest. Disneyland helped with the night photo. Frank's Custom Photo Laboratory in North Hollywood, Calif. is to be commended for fine photographic processing. Thanks also to Jane Osborn for the winter environment which made the snow photography feasible. And a special note of thanks to my wife Shirl for supplying the right doses of encouragement and patience that helped to meet the pressures of publication.